The Dreamer's Turn at the Fable

Nick O'Toole

BookLeaf Publishing
India | USA | UK

Presentation by *BookLeaf Publishing*

Web: www.bookleafpub.com

E-mail: info@bookleafpub.com

ISBN: 9789358737455

First edition 2023

For our fast-approaching baby,

you're about to enter the narrative

and start a new story, all your own.

ACKNOWLEDGEMENT

OK so obviously I have to acknowledge some inspirations. Matthew Stover for inspiring the way I look at stories. I also have to express my thanks to Al Ewing for Loki: Agent of Asgard, and to Neil Gaiman for The Sandman, both of which did a lot to shape my perspective on both stories and storytelling as I was entering my adult life. Without these authors, this book wouldn't have happened.

I want to acknowledge my family, who always keep me grounded, and who's excitement about my first book encouraged me to go again with a second one. More than that, I am grateful that they always encouraged me to make my own choices and form my own beliefs, regardless of if they clashed with theirs. If I couldn't trust them on that, this book couldn't have happened.

The circle of friends around me, boy howdy, you bet I acknowledge them. The time I get with you guys each week gives me something weekly to look forward to, and does wonders for my motivation. I'm incredibly excited to share these stories with you guys specifically. None of this is going to be One Piece, I'm not that good, but I hope you enjoy it at least a fraction that much. If I didn't think you'd like it, this book wouldn't have happened.

And above all of that, my darling wife, at this moment 27.5 weeks into carrying our baby, thank you for sticking by me. You got me to write my first book, and how could I possibly write a second one without that? You are all these things, my inspiration, my family, and my best friend. I love you so much, and without you, this book would not have happened.

PREFACE

In April of 2005, shopping in the Dymocks of the local Westfield, I bought a copy of Matthew Stover's novelisation of Revenge of the Sith. On the first page is a passage that has this to say:
"A strange thing about stories-
Though this all happened so long ago and so far away that words cannot describe the time or the distance, it is also happening right now. Right here.
It is happening as you read these words."
I was just about to turn twelve, and this passage changed the way that I would look at stories for the rest of my life. I'd never thought about the power and influence a reader could have over a world and its characters. How a story lives through being read and told to people, and how they die by being forgotten.

In 2014 I read Al Ewing's 17-issue comic, Loki: Agent of Asgard, an incredible look at the way stories shape characters- but also at how they constrain them. It features a reborn Loki trying to escape their role as the God of Evil by erasing the old legends about them, and replacing them with new legends to aspire to. It explored the metaphysics of narrative and character, and it gave me another layer to my own enjoyment of story and narrative.

You'll see inspiration from both of those in this book.

I love stories. Love hearing them, love telling them, always wanted to write them. I'm very excited to have this opportunity to write these stories down and have them released.

This book is built from two concepts that have been caught in my head for years.

The first concept is the idea of two entities of storytelling: one was the voice of the narrator, the quintessential essence of a voice telling you a story as you read it. The other one was the storyteller, who controlled the narrative and shaped it to a point. In this book they were simplified to be the Voice and Teller of Stories, and the first half of the book will have them telling a few short stories and hoping you'll enjoy them.

The second concept takes up the second half of the book and revolves around the way that stories shape our beliefs, and the power of storytelling in our conception of the afterlife.

What if someone with total control of the narrative wound up in a place entirely made from it? How would the characters in a story react to meeting someone who made the story happen. What if that character happened to be one of the most well-known villains in the history of mythology? And so came Lucifer, finally given a way to wage their war on Heaven without losing as the story dictates. The Dreamer's Turn at the Fable is a story that has lived in my head for a decade now, and I'm glad I finally got it out of there.

I hope you enjoy these stories. The Voice and the Teller are both very eager to be read.
Happy reading!

The Voice and Teller of Stories

An endless, countless time ago,
and also here and now,
there sits a figure robed in words-
a glint beneath their brow.

Suspended in a single point,
yet filling all of space.
A sentence-dressing paradox
that gazes at your face.

And with it's piecing gaze, what's this?
This feeling in your bones?
A sense this unfamiliar face
is one you've always known.

"Let me greet you, let me meet you,
let me see you then.
Sit a while, here in the narrative.
Drift in the prosaic eddies,
as they carry you through truth,
as they carry you through fancy,
as they carry you through possibility,
through potential, met and not."

Yes, there, familiarity!
a voice you've never heard-
yet one that's nested all your life
in each and every word.

You know them now, of course you do.
How could you not have known
The Voice Behind the Storytimes;
The constant, as you've grown.

And as you recognize The Voice,
a smile splits their cheek,
a captivating tone spills forth
and once again, they speak.

"Ah, you know me! Ah, you've met me!
Ah, you hear me, friend.
I invite you again to hear a tale,
To enjoy a fleeting yarn.
Let me spin for you an epic!
Let me spin for you a ballad!
Let me spin for you a shanty,
an adventure, grand or not!"

The Voice of Stories pauses now,
awaiting your reply,
a tale already on their lips,
the gleam still in their eye.

A story from the Voice themself?
Oh what a lovely treat!
What fortune favours you today,
that such a fate you'd meet?

And you're not going anywhere;
there's nowhere else to go.
Let's hear a story woven from
the greatest voice you know.

"Oh you'll hear me? Ah, you please me!
Yay, you honour me, friend.
Let me see now, what to tell?
How about a subtle one?
A story borne from intrigue,
A story borne from secrets,
A story borne from desires,
manipulation, good and not".

And as the Voice of Stories weaves,
another world is born.
Uncounted people, hopes and dreams,
experience their dawn.

The Voice creates a world per word,
each vibrant and each real,
all told with such a passion that
you couldn't help but feel.

See, that's the function of The Voice,
the purpose that it serves;
to give a story all the life-
the power- it deserves.

"Did you like it? Will you hold it?
Are you in it, then?
Will my story nest within you?
become part of your life tapestry?
Will my tale influence you?
Will my tale help inform you?
Will my tale live forever,
as a memory, a guide?"

I won't recall that story here;
it wasn't mine to tell.
Remember all the tales you've heard,
this one's in there as well.

Was it one that kept you warm at night?
Was it one that gave you pause?
Did it give you new perspectives?
or inspire you to a cause?

What lesson did you take from when
the Voice chose to regale?
For that's the strength of stories,
the power of the tale.

“So, another? Yes, another!
Aye, another, then!
I must insist upon another story!
My collection of words are belligerent-
They need your attention,
they need your contemplation,
they need your imagination,
a listener, a fertile audience.”

A story must be told, you see.
That’s Story’s only need.
To reproduce in sounds you hear,
on pages that you read.

Yes, even for the Voice of Stories,
all the rules are true.
They cannot help but beg to live,
to thrive inside of you.

Amazing, really, isn’t it?
They’re truly awesome things-
Yet stories crave an audience
to grow and spread their wings.

“Oh you’re here then? Ah, you too then.
Hmm, it’s you then.
I see you now, Story Teller.
I hear the riverbank of narrative.
Are you feeding me lines?

Are you feeding me ideas?
Are you feeding me at all?
Do I live, through your words?”

The Voice addresses me now,
they’ve noticed that I’m here.
and since I Tell the narrative,
The Voice is feeling fear.

See, if the Voice stops spinning yarn,
that story’s time will fail.
So too the Voice will disappear
if I don’t Tell their tale.

And I as well, the Teller,
I only live through you.
As soon as you stop hearing me,
my story will be through.

“We are the Voice, We are the Teller,
We are the Story.
We have some stories to give you.
Will you take them from us?
We have the power to craft worlds.
We have the strength to direct minds.
We have the ability to forge entire new realities
that will live with you forever”

But that’s only if you’ll hear us out.

Without you we grow frail.
We ask you, give our stories life.
Would you like to hear a tale?

A History of Rain and Storm

In the beginning, there was nothing
(Or maybe it was all there already?)
And all was dark
(Or maybe it was exceedingly bright?)
To be honest, it's vague.
Language was barely a zygote,
and you can imagine, I'm sure,
the trouble people had,
trying to shape stories
without the vocabulistic clay.

My story's first chapters
are spun like a glimmering web,
from shapeless threads of thought
(which never sit still long enough).
Nevertheless,
I'll try my best to recall them,
though you should be aware:
No spider weaves the same web twice.

Anyway.

In the beginning, there was (probably) nothing
And all was dark.
Until one day there was Thought.

And with Thought came Question.
And borne from Question, Reasoning.

The first thinking creatures noticed:
The skies sometimes darkened,
and following this,
everything got very wet.
And the thinkiest ones said,
“Things are not often wet.
Subverting the default dryness,
means something is at work”.

And so, floating in nothing
(save for the existential soup)
I took my first steps into form.
Here I was, here was I
brought forth through dreams.
Thrust into the world’s narrative
So some imaginative upstart
could have an answer for ‘rain’.

If I’m completely honest
(And really, why would I lie?)
I enjoyed being the Rain God.
Some of the other Gods
(we’ll get to them in time)
hate their jobs.
Not me though.
There’s a lot of variety in rain,

keeps the job exciting;
Today a few drops,
tomorrow a shower.
Now and then a drizzle,
if I'm feelin' cheeky.

They drew me onto cave walls
and I liked the body they gave me.
I evolved from a bundle of thoughts-
a nimbostratic puff-
into a shape much like them.
They say Man was Made in His Image,
but for most of us it's reversed.
I think you all find it easier
to imagine us like you.

They noticed, one day:
Things that often came with rain-
Thunder and lightning-
did not always come with rain.
Truthfully, I hadn't thought about it.
My job was making rain,
so I made rain.
The rest was neat coincidence.

Coincidence doesn't always work for them.

The debate began amongst them.
Some days they added to me;

now Rain and Lightning
and I could feel it in my winds.
The almighty power of lightning-
it was heady tonic.
But then there were other days,
I couldn't possibly be God of Two Things.
I was given terrible feelings,
like my guts were splitting,
as they pondered the possibility
that a Thunder God was born from me.
Other days I was made an infant
When they decided the reverse-
surely Rain was the child of Lightning?
After all, Lightning is so powerful
Thunder is so loud
and Rain is so gentle, it must be the youngest.
Perhaps we all were siblings?
The chaos was so much.

The chaos was too much.
I took some control of my story now,
tired of gaining power,
losing power,
gaining and losing family
to their rationalizing stories.
While they gave me the power,
I unleashed it all.
A torrent of Rain,
a shower of Lightning,

a cacophony of Thunder.
All at once, all together,
and unrelenting.

They developed a new understanding.
They put Rain, Lightning and Thunder
under an umbrella
and threw in Wind for good measure.
They now called me Storm.

I am not happy with my time as Storm.
Storm was not a fun God to be.
Rain had been gentle.
The cave drawings had all worn a smile.
But Storm was destructive.
Storm was cruel.

By this point they had developed discourse,
and through them my voice became haughty,
became imperious and overpowering.
At the behest of their narrative,
I sent the floods, I devised the hurricanes,
I annihilated whatever I saw fit.
At the time, it was my sick delight.

Their language developed,
and now they could spread their stories-
transmit them at any meeting point,
rather than on cave walls.

More and more people came to know Storm
And so Storm became more of me-
the part that had been Rain slipped,
stuck in those same cave walls.

I mentioned other Gods before-
There are a great many of us.
All of us children of Question and Reason,
crafted out of the same metaphysique.
Frankly, you people ask a lot of questions;
There's a God for everything.
"Where does rain come from?"
"What causes earthquakes?"
"Why is there a big glowy thing in the sky?"
I gotta tell you,
Sun Gods have it really easy.
"My job is to make sure the light stays on"
Yeah, OK, Mr Brightside.

Anyway at some point they realised,
"The Gods are not always at work.
They must have other lives.
They're just like me, for real".
So we all got social lives.

Difficult at first.
Hard to tell if it's worth the time
making friends with Fertility
when the ones telling your story

can decide that actually,
Storm gets on with Volcanoes,
obviously.
But eventually the chips fall.
Our friendships are forged,
our enmities engaged,
our stories grow beyond mere explanation.
No longer individual Gods.
Now, a Pantheon.

Before, Storms were just something I did.
They fell out of me,
literally like passing wind.
But now I was petty.
I would smite entire communities,
because they liked the God of Mangoes,
and he had hidden my favourite rock.
I would shake the sky with thunder,
as a mating signal
attempting to attract Revelry.
I would get drunk with Chaos and Abstraction
and in a haze
I would drown entire bloodlines.

I had to be careful, in some ways.
We had great power over the world,
But it was power they had given us
and they were always able to take it back
even if by accident.

I watched once as the God of Bears
(again, you have so many questions)
once unleashed an army of them,
just, hundreds of bears.
Bears hadn't realised though
All who had told his story
all lived in one place
and as his own bears devastated them
his story was forgotten.
The God of Bears unraveled then,
unspooled back into narrative thread.
Which, obviously, did not remove the bears.
The bears were now just there,
governed by nobody,
until someone else asked,
"What's the go with bears?"
and created a new story.

I got back to being Rain this way.
There had been an incredible argument.
Storm, Pestilence, Earthquake, Hellfire,
we all had something to say.
The world bore us,
the unfortunate scoreboard for our fight,
points etched into it by our dominions.
We were all hotheaded fools,
(especially Hellfire)
we destroyed more and more,

the collateral was our storytellers
and as the last of them were consumed
our stories could not be told
our powers collapsed into themselves.
And that would have been it.
except-

I imagined, in my final moments as Storm.
I imagined nonexistence approaching
and sent the gentle rain
to wash away our war
to repair what we'd done.

They reasoned afterwards,
that the rain was too gentle
too kind
to be counted under Storm.
Rain washed away the unwanted identity.
New Storm Gods were born
separate from me,
to handle that responsibility.
I got to be me again.

All of this was forever ago.
As populations spread, they mixed.
They met other people,
other questioners,
who had their own answers,
their own stories.

We met other Gods,
reflections of ourselves through concave
mirrors.
Pantheons met, mythologies combined.
I had a very long career as Rain.

All stories must end, however.

Mine is not quite over yet.
It just has much less power.
People stopped finding answers in Gods.
Their questions found other answers,
not in story, but in method.

Rain isn't my domain anymore.
Condensation, precipitation,
'The Water Cycle'-
they've taken my Godhood from me.
My story is only fiction now,
entertainment, rather than explanation.

Don't worry about it.
I had a really good innings.
More than most get.
And I live on in my story,
will live, as long as it gets told.

Thank you, for keeping me
The God of Rain
alive with you for a while.

Little Miss Muffet 2: Return of Miss Muffet's Revenge

"How are you, how be you,
how goes you?
It's me, I'm back again.
I never really left I guess.
Didn't leave you here,
didn't go anywhere,
didn't get out of the book,
can't be outside of the pages.

I'd like a turn, I need a turn,
it's now my turn.
I want to say a story this time.
It's about a kid I met one time,
She was a nice kid.
She was imaginative.
She was a funny kid
made me laugh, made me think.

Will you hear me, will you have me,
will you let me tell you?
I'll be here to say it all the same.
But it's up to you to listen.
Your choice to read it,
your choice to hear it,

your choice to hold it,
keep it, live it."

The story begins like this:

It was during a stroll through the park,
by the bigger pond.
A bit before you were born,
and half the world away.
That was a nice park, very green,
which is what you want in a park,
but not what you want in your bread.

"Although, I don't think that the ducks would mind."
came a voice.
I didn't think I'd said anything out loud-
although I'm told I speak a lot.
More than I think, anyway,
but then, I am the Voice of Stories.
Anyway, I looked away from the pond
and met eyes with a young girl.

I asked,
"Who are you, what to call you?
What's your story, friend?"
But she locked eyes on mine and said,
"I'm not your friend, we've never even met,
and strangers do not need to know my name!"

This is very wise thinking for a child,
proves her parents raised her right,
but I was out to collect a new story,
and this was very unhelpful.
"So I see, so you say,
so it is, my not-friend.
However, may I please address,
that you spoke to me first,
and I don't think you're strange."

She heard me out.
"You know a thing that real good friends would do?
they'd help me get back to my mum and dad.
I think, I think I lost them in the park
They'll think I'm lost and both be very sad."
and I thought,
What a thoughtful kid,
Here she is, doing fine,
being very wise,
and still finding room inside
to be worried about her parents.

But nice as the girl was,
The Voice of Stories isn't free.
"Sounds good that, how nice that,
let's do that then.
How abouts while we look for them,

You give me a good little story.
That I can pass on later,
that I can tell someone else,
that I can wrap up snug,
put in my pocket for safety."

"I still think you sound a little bit strange,
but okiedokie then, I'll tell you one:
I wonder if you've heard Miss Muffet Two?
I reckon that's a pretty awesome one."

Now I'm the Voice of Stories,
so obviously I've heard all the classics
and Miss Muffet goes way back.
I never knew it got a sequel,
and I couldn't wait to hear the follow-up.

"When last we saw Miss Muffet out to lunch,
she'd been attacked by a nasty, tricky Spider,
who had a devilish plan to take her food,
and spook Miss Muffet when he plopped beside
her.

But now, Miss Muffet's had beyond enough
of creepy crawlies taking all her snacks.
She says "I'll get that meanie Spider yet"
and starts to think of ways to get him back.

She thinks, and has a couple good ideas,

(She liked the one about the giant net)
but they all seemed so difficult and hard,
and needed tools she was too young to get."

We'd made it halfway around the park
and I was very excited.
What a fun narrative hook!
How would poor Miss Muffet
avenge her lost curds and whey?

"She asked her Mummy for some good advice,
what she would do, were she in Muffet's shoes,
and Mum said "Well, you know I practice law,
so if there's damage done, I guess I'd sue."

"But Muffet, dear, I've got no time for that.
I've got some work that's real and overdue."
So Muffet said "well, can I do it then?"
and Mother shrugged and said, "That's up to
you."

So Muffet went to school and studied hard,
applied herself and in a few short years,
she graduated out of lawyer school,
prepared to face the Spider she once feared."

A courtroom drama.
I couldn't believe my ears.
What a story.

I almost wanted it for myself,
to not share it with anyone.
But of course that wouldn't do-
what would we be doing then?

"She went to find the Spider after that,
to take his silly Spider butt to court,
and finally, she'd feast on curds and whey!
They'd taste the sweeter after all she'd fought.

ALAS! She hadn't thought to factor in
that spiders never seem to live that long.
Her foe had passed on many years ago;
She'd missed a chance to right the Spider's
wrong.

The Spider's kids had heard of Muffet's woes,
and said "Oh wait, he left a note behind."
So Muffet took the note and read it out,
and hearing it they all were shocked to find…

"For all the lunch I nicked across the years,
I truly wish that I could make it right.
I was a different, foolish spider then,
I thought the world was there for me to fight.

"Please take from me this true apology,
and all the lunches that I've ever stashed,
and just to help to sweeten up the deal,

I've also left a hundred bucks in cash."

So Muffet left the piles of whey and curds,
and chose to let the Spider's children be.
She took the hundred bucks in cash, of course,
and used it to pay off her college fee.

And after that, well I'm not really sure-
although I think I heard the people say
that when Miss Muffet got back home that night,
she finally had herself some curds and whey."

"So that's the end, and there's my Mum and
Dad!"

And indeed, we had found them.
The girl's parents seemed very intense
they asked me a lot of pushy questions.
But they seemed happy in the end.

I told the girl that I had loved her story.
When she said it was original work,
I was astounded.
I'd assumed she read Miss Muffet 2 elsewhere.
But I was glad to keep the story,
in one of my back pockets.

Before she left she told me her name
we weren't strangers anymore.

I have crossed her path a few times more,
which has done wonders for my collection.
Imaginative, like I said.

I'm not telling you her name though.
As she said,
strangers don't need to know.

"Okay then, alright then,
that's that then.
I hope you liked my little story!
I've got a few more if you'd like.
If you'd like to hear them,
if you'd like to enjoy them,
if you'd like to keep them,
give them somewhere to live?"

Diary of an Immortal Librarian

One day, while I was wondering,
I came across a man
from stories about Supermen
who flew around the land.

Some people there were super strong,
some used the elements,
and others did the weirdest things,
defying common sense.

Six hundred years he'd been around!
His power was to live.
He pushed a diary in my hand,
a story, his to give.

I believe he'd want it shared with you.

****

Dear Diary
I thought about quitting today.
It was feeling rote,
living in the library.
Four hundred years among books.

It feels a little pointless
seeing the kids
always doing new and exciting things.
I remember when being living fire
would have been spectacular
now it's barely even exciting.

But even the most common superpowers
are flashier than mine.
A healing factor and over-extended youth.
Can't make a name that way.
Which isn't a problem for me.
It's why I started the library
but even the oldest fogie,
the most stuck in my ways,
will wonder from time to time.

I didn't quit, of course.
David came to see me,
he said "Paul,
there ain't nobody else like you
who knows so much
about what was what."

It was a nice reminder,
without people like me
who actually lived it,
History would become a myth,

a place without form or reason.
It's my job to keep the story straight,
to keep the narrative in the lines.

People coming to the library
have people like David to thank.
People to remind us
why we are important,
and that everyone is.

****

Dear Diary
I find myself thinking about James,
James Collingham, to be precise.
The one from what used to be London.
I met up with him once,
after he'd been gone for thirty years.

He'd run off to Who Knows Where,
after a huge row with his mum.
Of course she was hurt,
but,
surprising to most of his family,
(though not to anyone close),
she was not as hurt as us.
Mrs Collingham never missed him
near as much as us.

But thirty years on, he found me
with my then-wife Louanne.
It was easy, he said.
"You've barely changed".
And truly, compared to the years on his face,
the seconds on mine
must have stood out.

He'd known right away
what I have ended up being.
Turns out he'd been abroad,
helping to make homes for people.
People like me,
becoming strange and new.
People like him,
who needed a place to be.

People like me were rarer then,
we existed on the fringe,
because when we dared otherwise
there was…
pushback.
I was lucky, very lucky,
that I could pass back then.

Louanne was not like me
she lived a normal sixty-eight years
and we got fourty-four of them together.
She never blamed me

(as a lot of others have)
for staying young forever.
"Paul, you've always had an old soul, anyway",
she would say to me.
It somehow took some decades more
before I understood that.

James had been the opposite.
Here he was at fourty-seven,
a much younger man behind his eyes.
Eyes that were probably brown,
but I remember them as amber.

We'd only had that afternoon
but I remember him now
vividly
as a question I have to ask myself.
James Collingham saved lives
for thirty years.
So what have I done then,
with the last six-hundred?

****

Dear Diary
I miss my Darcy.
eighty years was most lifetimes,
(though only part of hers),

but still I wanted more.
In two-hundred years,
I'd had a few wives.
But after two-hundred and fifty,
I couldn't take another.

I've lost most of my time with Louanne.
I hope it's not calloused to say,
but be fair to me;
six hundred years is a lot of people,
and most of them haven't lasted.

Darcy should be out there somewhere.
I hope I would know if she'd passed.
She was a hundred and eighty
when I knew her,
and not a day older than twenty.
We were enjoying freedom together,
in times when people like us
were becoming more frequent.

She'd love to live they way we do now.
She'd used to ask,
"How do these 'normal' people
how do they think they can?
How do you litigate superpowers?
The world needs catching up, Paul."

So yes, I like to think she is,

happy to know that people like us
are everywhere.
Part of me hopes she has a family,
though part of me hopes the opposite,
that she was smart enough to not.
I always knew I couldn't outlive a child.

I think it was our shared love of learning
that brought us together.
I always loved cataloguing the world,
she always loved living in it.
When the world rebuilt itself again,
while I was taking notes,
collecting artifacts,
she was with the people,
making sure there were notes to take.

Of course, the differences there
eventually led us apart.
Well, led her away really.
I was already mired in my library,
and so I stayed.

I think Darcy's better suited to this
to the long-lived thing.
learning the world as it happens,
instead of waiting for it to pass into history.
That's why I like to picture her alive,
not waiting for me to archive her

like I have for so many others.

****

Dear Diary,
I saw another Everyman today.
Another one who seems to have it all.
Who can fly,
Who can punch real good,
Who apparently can't be hurt.
And probably all kinds of other tricks.

They show up now and then
every few decades or so.
They're all so ready,
so ready to be Him.
The next Everyman.
But they aren't Him, trust me,
I knew the first one.

Everyman is an easy myth.
He only showed up once,
and beat back the end of the world.
It took his life to do it.
The Legend Writers had the one real event,
and got to fill in the rest.

The Everyman in real life
was young,

barely a fraction as old as me.
And as the world crashed around him
like the rest of us
he was shaking on the ground.
Like me, I assume,
wondering if this was where I'd finally die.

But Lily from down the road?
Now there was a legend.
A proper hero.
She's the one who told him.
"Everyman, you're immortal.
The rest of us aren't.
Will you still hide from ghosts
when all of us are dust?"

Lily was a good kid.
It's strange what we remember.
She used to feed the ducks
at the pond that once was Percy's.
Lily from down the road smiled then,
and took his hand.
"We all deserve to be better,
to make a new world
where you wouldn't have to hide.
But you're the only one
who can give us the chance."

The Everyman became a legend.

Lily had been right.
His story became immortal,
and the world
having dodged a bullet,
moved on.

These new Everymen that show up
I wonder who their Lily was?
Do they even have one?
Or am I the only person
with a Lily from down the road,
living in their head?

****

Dear Diary,
I think I'm using you wrong.
I think, if I'm right,
You're meant to be about my life.
Preserve my history.

But I'm six hundred and thirty two,
and just got my first grey hair.
So I'll be able to tell my story
for at least a while yet.

When you're full, I'll archive you.
Give you your own special place,
the pride of all my library.

I hope that you get read.

Dear Diary, it’s your job now,
to save their stories instead,
to keep them alive
in the moments between your pages.

The Non-King's Greatest Treasures

"We met a man, we know a man,
we saw this man once.
A perfectly average fellow,
but one with a story nevertheless.
A story about purpose,
a story about success,
a story about a life lived,
a good one, a proud one."

He'd worn a pair of cargo shorts,
his shirt a browny-red.
And as he talked he always wore
a smile on his head.

He said this:

I own no castles.
I hold no vast riches,
command no subjects,
and the opportunity to own land
will almost certainly evade me forever.
Yet by my metrics
(the only ones I care for),
I live as a King.

What else would you call it?

I pursue good crafts,
I eat good food,
I make good sport,
and I do it all in excellent company.

What better thing is there,
than being in a room with your people?
To joke and laugh,
to make merriment?
What more could one want
than to appreciate another life
to enjoy your similarities,
learn from your differences?
Build each other up,
and know in turn
that you are appreciated?

I recall mere weeks ago,
we sat round a fire.
They discussed stories from their youth
and I listened, pretending to read a book.
I would quip responses and insights.
(The kinds of things
that have annoyed people before.)
How nice then to be with friends,
who instead appreciate it,

and even join in.
How delightful to trust in company.
We all had our challenges going on,
demons at the door.
But at the door we checked them,
and from our shared fire
we all drew a bit of light,
to pick the demons up again.

What a fantastic thing,
to be enchanted thus,
a magic against the dark.

Sporting has been my engagement
'ere I was a tiny wee thing,
inspired by grand stories,
by tales of incredible duels
and the kings who fought them.
The sport itself, a fresh story every time,
a narrative that opened, had conflict, and ended
but which unfurled uniquely whenever it was
told.
And in this,
I became a very skilled narrator.
(in this alone though-
I tried my hand at writing,
and my hand was found wanting).

It was here that I made an excellent friend.

We met in clean competition,
a warm day, a pleasant breeze
(although later that grew into a storm).
He talked to me before we matched-
no familiarity in his head,
no prior meetings between us-
we became fast friends
before we even took up arms.
I don't recall which of us won,
(although if it was me,
I probably wouldn't forget it)
but after we met for a meal.
In the many years since,
we have sparred often,
each keeping sharp,
so as not to disappoint the other.

This is a true friendship,
one that builds its participants up,
and is enjoyable to both.

Now food, there's an interesting one.
You can clearly see
(or so I assume)
that I take delight in cuisine.
Most people do.
And yet, there are many,
(many men especially)
who say that success means

not having to cook for oneself.
Which proves, I think
that my metrics for success
are the most correct ones.
Afterall it is a delight,
to dance in the tastes and flavours,
to sing along to the fragrance
of heat applied to meat and veg.

A meal is a great way to make friends.
Tongues unwind with taste on their tips,
and sitting around the table
we shared in some mixed savouries.
Twas on a short cruise,
we were drifting downriver
on our way to watch the games.
She made a fuss about needing salt,
and I was displeased.
I cooked the fish myself,
and as a good cook does,
I had salted it before cooking.
Aye, I was a wee bit miffed
that my fish wasn't good as was.
However,
as a good cook does,
I provided as was requested.

The salt was placed on the table
and there it stayed

the whole ride through.
I must admit,
I had one eye on it the whole time.
I finally asked her why
and she replied,
"A table is so incomplete
without the appropriate dressing,
don't you think?"
And I laughed then,
laughed at my own insecurities,
and laughed with joy,
for this peculiarity was delightful.
Over time I found that she was full of them.
Endless charming foibles.

A true mark of a well-lived man,
making sure his friends can eat,
whatever and whenever they please.

Now for myself,
I practice my crafts-
smithing being a big one.
Countless hours have I spent,
learning to manipulate shapes,
honing my sense of the materials.
My triumph over form and function,
though still a lofty goal,
moves more in reach with every day.
The pursuit keeps me grounded,

and each successful progress
is marked as a success.
The skills can always sharpen,
and I am fulfilled by the act.

And there's practicality
in being able to smith.
Those same friends of mine
can be spotted by my work.
By the trinkets I share with them.
I don't sign those pieces,
But I know
I take great pride in seeing them used.
and they know
they do me a service by appreciating them.
I have seen my friends take my work with them,
a part of my history gone with them,
just as their trust goes with me.

If such personal fulfillment
does not mark a life of success,
then I must pity the successful.

Again, I say to you:
I have no castle, no gold, no subjects
but I mark my days in good times
and even better friends,
and by any reasonable measure,
it is a king's life.

And on his way, he went.

The man in browny-red went on,
we watched him on his way.
He left with us a story trope
we use until today.

"It's a good trope, quite a nice trope,
It's a trope that gets good use.
That not-king left a story-beat behind,
about the value of a good cast of characters.
The real story's in the people.
The real story's in relationships.
The real story, the real treasure,
was the friends you made along the way."

Hunting the Warradango

"It's a big world, it's a large world,
it's a great world out there.
Full of all kinds of wonderful creatures.
They make for wonderful stories.
Creatures who are majestic.
Creatures who are frightening.
Creatures who inspire greatness,
imagination, and wonder."

There is a mountain with three peaks,
one with its head in the clouds,
one just above them,
and one that sits ever below their sight.
This mountain has a name
in a language forgotten to time
but its translation, roughly done, is
Mount Eternal Struggle of Siblinghood.
I remember the translation,
because I never had siblings,
and found it very difficult to wrap my head
around.

Anyway
I was on the Three-Peaked Mountain,
having a wonder around,

As you do,
and I noticed a collection of berries.
They grew on a thin-stemmed plant
and had a delightful blue-red colour.
Not purple, mind,
the colours were not mixed,
but instead complimentary,
dancing along the berry's skin.
Having not seen such a fruit before,
a rarity for me, having been on lots of mountains,
I elected to give it a try.
And because I am not a savage,
rather than indelicately plucking the stems,
I took one from a convenient basket,
which was sitting not far away,
next to a small, unlit fire.

Well, the berry was delightful.
They were crisp-skinned,
so they made a delightful pop,
and they tasted of knowledge and insight.
It's an excellent taste,
but one I tend to avoid.
Both flavours pair unkindly with narrative.

While I was enjoying the berry,
there appeared a man,

holding a very sharp stick,
and wearing a very angry face.
He spoke in the old language of the mountain,
and in shorter detail it became clear
that I had trespassed on his basket
and if I could not replace the berry
we would both face the wrath
of the Warradango.

This was the wrong appeal to make.
As I like to collect stories,
so too did I like to collect creatures.
and this Warradango was intriguing,
as it was supposedly wrathful,
in spite of its fun name.
So while I could have replaced the berry,
if I did the story wouldn't continue.
I instead sat myself down,
and waited to meet it.
Which apparently was not how it worked.
The man with the stick collected the basket,
quite forcefully insisting
that I go with him.
I had nought else to do,
so I went with him.

The man, turns out, was from a village.
He took his berry basket,
and offered it to a woman.

She was somehow unlike him,
in more ways than just gender.
She took the basket and spoke,
"Only twenty-nine berries here.
The order was set at thirty."
The stick-man clearly hoped she wouldn't count
and truthfully, she didn't.
But she'd eaten the fruit of knowledge and
insight,
and didn't need to count to quantify.
"You ate the forbidden fruit?"
she was speaking to me now.
And while my Voice is of Stories,
it is not one for lies.

"I took it, I ate it,
I liked it a lot.
Thank you very muchly for the chance!
I see you also-"

"Silence, tall one!
You have broken a vow.
One twixt myself and the beast.
Silence you, or see the wrath
of the Warradango!"

I looked expectantly left.
I looked hopefully right.

But no creature did appear.
No Warradango,
only this lady,
and several followers cowering.

“I don’t see it. Should I see it?
Do I get to see it then?”
The lady in the middle was shocked
which seemed odd to me,
as did the whole situation.
“Is the Warradango not coming?
Seems rude, to make a threat
and not follow through.
Seems inconsistent.”

She glanced left at the others.
“As the speaker for the Warradango,
the mighty and wrathful Warradango,
I’ll admit to some surprise.
Such a novel desire.
I will admit then to a bluff.
In speaking to the Warradango
in the chill of early morning,
they told me that they will not be out today,
electing for a day of rest.
Take the chance now then stranger,
and continue on your way.”

But I was piqued in interest now.

"What way then does it rest?
I want to see it,
'ere I head home."

She considered me,
and rather helpfully,
she said that I would need to head,
out to the tallest peak,
where the air became thin,
and in the deepest of the night
I may spot the Warradango.
She requested also,
that should I see the white ottermine,
to bring it back to her
that she might have its excellent coat.

So I climbed to the top of the tallest peak,
the eldest sibling,
if I understand the metaphor.
It was the kind of trip
that would have been harsh,
if I were not able to simply tell myself there.
It was mid-winter,
and I was forced to keep myself warm,
which I did by remembering good stories,
of lovely friends I had met.

The Warradango must also have been cold,
because they did not appear,

not even as I whispered to the mountain,
"pretty please".

I did meet the ottermine though,
her coat was astounding indeed.
She sold it to me
for three ballads and a soliloquy.
Warmest piece of clothing I ever wore.

The Speaker for the Warradango
had clearly been rooting for me,
as she was disappointed when I returned,
unenlightened by the trip.
However I gave her the coat,
because a gentleperson keeps their promises.

She told me that I must have just missed it.
Mere hours after I had first left,
the Warradango had arrived here.
It had punished the man with the stick,
clearly it had needed that extra berry I took.

I asked if there was anywhere else it would go.
I was still curious,
and now I had to apologise for eating its food.
She told me that the Warradango,
terrifying Warradango,
would sometimes head to the shortest peak.
It was scheduled there in three days time,

to hold council with the other animals.
There were deadly animals out there,
with teeth and claws that made for excellent tools,
but with danger enough to be unworth the risk.
I made for it at once.

This was an easier trip,
but less pleasant;
the youngest sibling was eclipsed by clouds,
leaving its majesty hidden unless one looked hard.
There was a large, circular clearing
perfect for a parliament,
and many of the foretold animals approached
as I waited out the three days.
They came with teeth and claws,
and bartering with good fables,
I built a small collection to take back.
Animals like these were far too clever
to attack a Voice of Stories.
Still, the three days came and went
and I even waited a fourth,
but clearly the Warradango
had nothing to make council about.

When I returned this time,
to the very unhappy Speaker,
I handed over the teeth,

but elected to keep the claws.
Afterall, I was starting to feel put out.
"I'm wondering if I'll ever see
this Warradango for myself."

The Speaker's followers murmured agreement,
clearly also disappointed for me.
And after hearing this,
the Speaker made an offer.
"The Warradango makes a main home
with the middle peak,
with the head in the clouds.
We shall go together,
you, me, and my murmuring followers.
I shall speak to the Warradango,
and you all shall see."

It was a longer trip,
walking with people,
not at the speed of story.
The clouds around the middle sibling
were thick, white,
and carried their share
of rain and mystery.

Our troop kept shrinking.
One day we found two missing-
the Speaker had sent them back for supplies.
The next three more were gone-

the Speaker said they'd fallen.
In days to come we dwindled.

One night I found her awake.
I told her I had to return home,
which was true.
I can't be away forever.
I would just hope to see
the Warradango
a different time.

"There is no Warradango,
which I'm sure you well know."
she said.
"You're not from here, I know.
I'm not from here either."

Well now that was disappointing.
It was all a ruse?
But it was also intriguing.
Where was the Speaker from?
and what did she speak to, then?

"I come from a different time.
One where we have killed all our myths,
logicked them into myth.
On a dare, I came here
to see if I could make a new myth.
These people were ready to believe one,

and so I made one to serve me.

I got stuck here though.
Stranded.
I collected the berries hoping for insight,
hoping to go home.
I had to make them forbidden-
I was upon a throne of secrets,
you know?
And the people starting to doubt-
well they won't make it home from here.
The Warradango will have gotten them all.
So sorry to disappoint you."

But was it disappointing?
Nay!
I had missed out on a new creature, sure.
"But instead I found a new villain!
A manipulator, a schemer!
People like you make for such excellent stories!"

I thanked her and turned,
to whisk myself home,
amid some vague reprimand or threat.
I truly wouldn't have paid attention,
except that it stopped abruptly-
one of the remaining sleepers had woken
and seemingly, they had better places to be.
I mean, they must have been better,

because the Speaker ran right after them,
into the middle sibling's fog.

So, I went home.
No new creature to share with the Teller,
but a new archetype to build from.
Hardly a wasted trip.
Of course,
No good story is wasted time.

The One Beyond the Last

Inside the ruins of his shed,
a builder sat alone.
His back-of-home robotics lab
was into chaos thrown.

His name was Alan Turington,
Machine Extraordinaire,
and he'd been building robots with
a keen and eager flair.

He specialised in little droids,
no higher than his knee.
He programmed them for friendship
and to keep him company.

The first of them he'd built at ten.
at twelve, built number two.
And so it went for twenty years,
his favourite thing to do.

His robots burned through energy,
so quickly fell apart.
But what they gave while functioning
was joy to Alan's heart.

And when they burned their battery out,
it pained him to the core
but that had never stopped him yet
from simply building more.

Some years of good companionship,
weighed up against the pain,
had often seemed to Alan like
a trade he'd make again.

But every time a robot died,
hurt harder than before.
And when the last one flickered out,
then Alan thought, 'no more'.

"My heart won't take another one"
he'd told himself that day.
"No short successes, all too brief,
before they're wiped away."

Which brings us to the ruined shed,
which Alan tore apart;
"I can't rebuild another one
if I've nowhere to start."

Then in the dark and misery,
the man began to weep.
But that was interrupted by
a small but vocal "beep".

From underneath a toppled shelf,
askew against the wall,
from out of rubble thrown about,
a little robot crawled.

A long-forgotten prototype
from Alan's early days
Who's maintenance and turning on
had fallen by the ways.

Her chassis was a smaller one,
and rather incomplete,
but still she slowly moved to him
on little robot feet.

In silence Alan watched her come.
He watched as she explored,
unable then to stop himself
he scooped her from the floor.

And looking at her little head,
her lightly glowing eye,
his declaration was forgot
and he began to cry.

He couldn't leave this robot here,
he couldn't shut her down.
He'd do his best and fix her up-

this robot that he'd found.

He found that she was curious,
observing as he worked,
with wonder at the oddest things-
a charming little quirk.

Among the cache of bits and bobs
still littering the lab,
he pulled together everything
there was in reach to grab.

He worked himself into the night
to fix the little bot
and as the dawn came overhead
he looked at what he'd got.

Her motors got a tuning up,
her joints were limbered too.
And with new legs she tested out
the things that she could do.

He'd powered up the subroutines
that helped her learn and think.
He let her pick a paint job out,
and she chose blue and pink.

The thing that she liked most of all,
the brand new sense of touch,

fulfilled her curiosity
of things that she could clutch.

He couldn't find a voicebox though,
nor build her one from scratch,
but barring that he'd done the job
and everything was patched.

She hopped around on brand new legs
and beeped a happy beep,
and Alan found himself resigned,
because he knew she'd keep.

The little robot that he'd fixed
was grateful, he could tell.
"I guess, I guess it couldn't hurt
to love this one as well."

He named the little robot "Leaks",
because her oil dripped.
No matter what he tried, her tank
would always seem to slip.

But she was good, so never mind.
As far as Alan saw,
he wasn't here to stress about
a very minor flaw.

Together they rebuilt the lab

although they left it cold.
"It isn't time, not ready yet.
perhaps when we get old".

A cheerful robot, was our Leaks,
exploring all the world,
content to just enjoy her time
and see how it unfurled.

And Alan treasured all their time,
as every moment passed.
Miss Leaks made Alan's heart come back,
the one beyond the last.

The Sour Grapes of Villainy

A man called Vincent Lainey once,
met with us on the road,
and said that we had done him wrong
and recompense was owed

"A funny man, a handsome man,
a man from out of stories.
We'd given him a Voice inside a tale.
We'd cast him as the villain then,
A villain to oppose the hero,
a villain to cause conflict,
a villain to enhance the story,
give it life, a lasting power."

We asked of Vincent Lainey then,
"So what's all this about?"
This character had pains with us
and we would hear him out.

Vincent's story was this:

Imagine, if you will,
twisting the narrative ether
clutching the shapeless words,
dressing them up in shape and form,

gifting it a life,
a name (Vincent Lainey),
building them a backstory
and then telling him,
"You are the villain of the story".

A bit unfair, I reckon.

Assume you had a baby.
conceived in reality,
born to a real life.
And you told them,
"No hopes and dreams for you!
You're a mechanic, kid.
Here's your overalls,
your toolkit,
and a big ol' blob of grease!"
and then dared to be shocked
when they grew up to fix a car.

Nothing against mechanics, to be clear.
Just making a point,
that enforcing roles on people
is generally not OK,
and maybe characters like me
deserve the same respect.

You told my first story,
so many years ago,

and I guess I should be thankful.
A child doesn't remember
what their infancy was like.
Perhaps being born at forty
and having it encoded in story
has helped in that regard.

You said that I was charming,
that I was smart
that I was well-liked.
But there was someone that you liked more.
Richard Type.
So I became mean-
a bully-
and vile insecurities,
from a childhood I never had,
overshadowed those qualities
so your favourite would look better.

Made me sneer to make him smile,
made me harsh to make him gentle,
made me manipulate, so he could stay honest.
And it wasn't even subtle.
For goodness' sake,
you called me V. Lainey!
I changed overnight
as you'd planned from the start.

Can you imagine being defined

by your opposition to one person?
Can you imagine
Having no desires,
speaking no words,
dreaming no dreams,
except when those would be a mirror
to show the hero how good they are?

And obviously, I fought with him.
What else was I to do?
This upstart
who thought he was so great,
so cool,
was in my way.
And of course,
inevitably,
I was beaten
as the story demands.

That could have been the end of it.
Could've taken my licks
and moved on.
Maybe could've had a life.
But no,
I was too popular.
no escape for me.

You made a sequel,
forced me back,

this time with brand new plans-
revenge I didn't even want,
not really,
until suddenly I needed it.
The plot demands
And I, Vincent Lainey
am but her humble servant.

You'd reckon twice would be enough
But uh-oh!
oopsie-daisy!
I was a fixture now,
The audience had gotten hold
and made me vital,
an unremovable piece,
a load-bearing beam
of Richard Type's story.

And now I couldn't even hate him.
I realised after that,
that much as everything I was
was there to make him Rich,
he was also tied to me.
He smiled to make me sneer,
he was gentle to make me harsh,
he was honest, so that I could deceive.

A hero without a villain

is just a guy.
A good guy, probably,
but nobody cares about Just A Guy.
Stories need conflict, don't they say?

So no.
I couldn't hate him.
The most I had was pity.
Pity and a wish to free him.
By ending him,
I'd be free as well.

Here I was, then.
A villain
desperate to defeat a good man,
who I had no desire to beat.
Just a horrible drive
thrust onto me by narrative.

I met with Rich eventually.
Over coffee, we talked.
He asked me why I did what I did.
I told the truth.
"I can't stop at this point".
And he nodded,
he understood.
But not everything.

"Why do you hate me, Vin?"

and of course I had no answer.
What was I meant to say?
'I hate the way I can't be you'?
'I hate that good comes so easily,
while I'm stuck in the mud'?
'I hate this endless battle'?
All these things were true,
but none of them were about him.
I hated our circumstance,
but never Richard Type.

And so again, I told the truth,
as much to myself as him.
This was the first time I truly owned it.
The first time I let myself reckon.

"I envy you, Richard.
Everyone admires you,
and I'm one of them.
But I'll never get to be like you.
Not as long as we live."

I think he got it.
He looked at me
with the same pity I felt for him.
A kindred spirit,
the other side of a symbiotic coin.

We both deserved a life,
a life without the other.
It seems only fair,
most people get one.
But try as might
I couldn't think of how.
I hadn't been born to do a good deed.
I was here to be a villain.
And in the end that was it.
I had to be a villain,
to act as villains do.

I forced our final conflict.
I kidnapped his girlfriend,
as was the style at the time.
Something would end today,
whether it was her,
or him,
or me.

It was me.
It was never going to be the girl.
I had no grudge.
We fought our final battle then,
Vin and Rich,
a battle for the ages.
He tried to let me live, in the end.
But I could not.
And as a villain does,

I took another swing at him,
and the retaliation got me.

And finally,
the thought I had was peace.
I wouldn't get my own story,
but at least I wasn't stuck in his.

It lasted for a while this time.
afloat in the stream of consciousness,
not worried about anything,
or anyone,
or vengeance,
or measuring up to anyone,
or Richard Type.

Until

Some utter genius,
inspired by your story,
decided it needed adapting!
And so,
the stream of consciousness was bottled
and I was poured right back into the role,
except at the start again.

And the whole damned thing began again!

It was a cycle,

a recursive entrapment.
Our battle for the ages
became one for the books,
then one for the radio dramas,
Then one for the screen.

And so often the cycle turned
that sometimes I even liked it.
There was comfort in the recursive.
And so many voices spoke my words,
so many faces wore my thoughts,
I liked at least some of them.

But on and on it goes.

I have to wonder now,
will our story ever get to end?
Or will I be the villain forever?
Forced to hate and scheme,
forever made to fight a foe,
who by now
was the most steadfast presence I knew,
the only constant good,
while all else would change around me.

I come here not to curse you,
for making me this way.
You are the Voice and Teller,
and simply do your function-

but please
I want to be free of villainy.
I deserve a chance for change.

And so did his appeal end.

"We considered it, we thought on it,
we mulled it over in our heads.
It was an unconsidered consequence for us.
For truly we never intend to cause harm.
What could we do for him?
What could we change for him?
What could we do to find him peace,
some freedom, a life his own?"

We have a trick for times like this,
we've used it ever since.
There's power in identity,
and his would need a rinse.

We changed his face, we changed his name,
and with it he was free.
No more would Lainey trouble him,
no villain would he be.

So now when stories grow too big,
and start to take a toll,
The Voice and Teller have a way
to free them from the role.

The Dreamer's Turn at the Fable: Chapter Zero, Preludes and Introductions

"Hey there, hi there,
hello there.
It's me! I'm back again!
How've you been liking things so far?
Hope you've had a good time,
hope you've enjoyed our stories,
hope you're ready for a big one now,
one with parts, one with chapters!

Let's talk about chapters.
A lot of little stories,
that team up to tell a whole.
How very exciting!
It's like,
a story version of a sport team.

We're always very excited,
when we get to tell a story in chapters.
What you're about to get
is one of our first ever.
One we've told before,
and one we'll tell again,

as many times as we're asked.

This story is about a story,
one I'm sure you've heard about.
About the ever recurring clash
between Hell and Heaven,
and the one making it all happen.
It's a story like all good stories,
like any good story about gods and legends,
it happened forever ago,
and it happened yesterday.
It could happen next week.
Legends are constantly happening,
because they are always being told.

It's a small cast.
a minimal Dramatis Personae.
We have
-Lucifer, The Fallen One, Lord of Hell.
You probably have an idea of them.
-God, the Heavenly and Holy.
You definitely know who He is.
-The Dreamer, our Main Character.
She has a name,
but we're keeping it secret,
for reasons that should become clear.
Instead we call her
The Dreamer,
and we're going to leave at that.

This is our story
and it is the Dreamer's story,
and while you read it
it is also your story,
to enjoy as you please.

It happened long ago,
it will happen again,
and it is happening now,
as you read these words;
it happens inside your head.
Thank you for giving it the space.

The Voice and Teller of Stories invite you to:

The Dreamer's Turn at the Fable.

Chapter One: Meeting Saint Peter Above the Clouds

The sky that day was beautiful,
a deep and lovely blue,
the kind of sky that hits just right,
the perfect kind of view.

The weather was inspiring,
the temperature just right,
the kind that people sing about
and makes a person bright.

But none of that means anything,
it hasn't any worth,
because we're at the Pearly Gates
and no longer on Earth.

The Dreamer stood in line to wait,
surprised at what she saw.
"For real? Am I in line for Heaven now?
Well this is something I'm not ready for.

I thought it must've been a fairy tale,
a pleasant story, what else could it be?
But hey, the pudding has the proof I guess.
There's egg upon my face for sure, that's me."

That morning she'd been slow to move,
awoke from deepest sleep
by noises from her old alarm,
the ever-present beep.

She'd dreamed about a peregrine,
that wore a golden crown,
and aiming to expand on that,
she quickly wrote it down.

It joined the little notebook that
she kept beside her bed,
for all the tales and stories that
found life inside her head.

And this was how it always was,
e'er since she was a kid.
Creating little stories was
just simply what she did.

But clearly something had gone wrong,
to be at Heaven's gate,
without a sense of how it was
she'd met with such a fate.

"You'd think, I think, the way you died would be
a thing that you'd remember after all.
Not knowing how my story ended, well,

I'll say, I'm just a little bit appalled."

The person in the line before
did turn and shake their head.
"I tell you what, I hate that I
know how and why I'm dead.

Be grateful for the silence mate,
for ignorance is bliss.
I truly wish I didn't know
how I had come to this."

"I cannot stand an open-ended tale.
I can't move on without a proper end."

The Dreamer did this all the time,
before to death she'd passed.
In her world ambiguity
was not allowed to last.

If stories hadn't ended well,
she soon took care of that.
a story had to finish up,
and that was where she sat.

And after all, the kids at work
would simply not accept
to book that closed before it ends
would truly be inept.

"I think it's nice," the person said,
"that yours is still unknown.
without it written down on rock,
you get to write your own."

The Dreamer reconsidered this,
and didn't quite agree,
but didn't want to argue what
an unknown death could be.

She let the line continue on,
'I wonder what it was that did me in,'
a thought she kept inside her head,
'I wonder how my afterlife begins.'

But though she tried, and though she thought,
it wouldn't come to mind,
'til finally she'd just accept,
and push it back behind.

And just in time she made the choice;
she'd made it to the front.
A guy behind a giant desk
waved over with a grunt.

"So you must be Saint Peter, if I'm right.
I think the story says you check the list?"
The guy fixed up his glasses with

a flicker of his wrist.

"Yes, that's right, very good.
It's one of the most commonly known
stories about Heaven,
and you got it in one go."

Which came across as rather rude,
and not at all okay.
'But then again, it can't be all that fun,
and I would guess it's been a lengthy day.'

"Hey thanks so much for being here, Saint Pete.
It's cool you're here to show us where to go.
I haven't read my bible in a while,
the etiquette is stuff I wouldn't know."

Saint Peter laughed a bit at that,
he'd clearly been disarmed.
The Dreamer was a friendly one,
and Peter liked her charms.

"Look thanks for your acknowledgement,
I see a lot of souls in a day,
and it's easy to forget
that you haven't been here before.
Let's start over."

Saint Peter took and shook her hand,

the two exchanged their names.

“So as you’ve guessed,
I’m here to check your file.
See if you’re through the gates,
or if it’s down below.
And I’ll be honest,
the latter would be a bummer for us both.”

The Dreamer felt so nervous then,
as all do who are judged.
Saint Peter tallied up her life-
she didn’t dare to budge.

“It’s looking pretty good here.
No major sins,
no puppies kicked.
You’ve got a knack for storytelling,
that’s always fun.
It says you work with children,
already a gold star,
and not a single one of them
has or ever will have a mean thing to say.”

This helped the Dreamer’s teeth unclench,
as good reviews will do.
“When you say ‘has or ever will’, you mean-“

“Sharp ear, that.

You're used to linear time, I guess.
Time is funky here.
Our records span entirety,
from the start to the end.
Helps us to really judge your impact,
for accurate results."

"Anyway, your file is fine,
and you seem pretty nice.
Unfortunately there's one issue."

She wondered what she must have done,
how major was the crime?
She wracked her brain but couldn't tell
which sin would earn her time.

"The file says you don't believe,
not in our holy God.
Non-belief is a pretty big red flag,
something you'll find with
pretty much the entire afterlife."

"I've always just assumed it was a fable,
like every other story that I've read,
and thinking that, I wasn't really able
to trust there'd be a life when I was dead."

Saint Peter nodded. "Not ideal,
but also not that rare.

My job expanded recently,
with atheism's rise.
If you just show me some faith now,
I can fix the record up,
and we're on our way in."

"So will I get at least to meet Him then?
I wouldn't hate to meet the myth Himself."

"Well, He doesn't come out here.
You need to go in first.
So you need to have faith.
Also, please don't call Him a myth."

"You mean we have to go in fully blind?
You need the faith to come from nothing else?"

"Yes, that's the long and short.
quickly now please,
I can't give you all day
for a crisis of belief.
Let's go."

"I mean, the gates are literally right there.
You're telling me He can't just say hello?
You could be telling any other tale,
or any story, far as I would know."

"It's not a case of knowing.

You trust me or you don't.
Last chance now."

"I just don't think it's very fair at all,
demanding faith while under threat of Hell.
Manipulative is what I'd say it is,
and insecure, as far as I can tell."

Saint Peter shrugged and stamped the file,
"Unfortunate," he said.
"But if that's what you're going with,
my hands are tied."

"Please enjoy damnation"

And so the Dreamer fell.

Chapter Two: Hell is Endless Admin Work

There's many paths that merge to make
the highway into Hell,
As multi-laned and numerous
as every soul that fell.

The Dreamer fell for quite a bit,
and not that long at all,
and when she landed, found herself
within an admin hall.

"Awaiting judgement in a line again?
I will admit, it sounds like Hell to me."

But as more lanes were open here,
the line was much more fast,
and so she reached the front of it
before much time had passed.

Behind a little folding desk
an orange person sat,
who's posture and a furry face
was like a crouching cat.

"Good morning,

thanks for waiting,
our deepest apologies for the line,
unless you're an actual evil person,
in which case,
sorry the line wasn't longer,
you underbaked cumquat."

It was the Dreamer's turn with that
to be the one disarmed.
"We demons speak our minds down here,
no need to be alarmed.

Don't worry about it either,
your file got here long before you did.
No belief in God, hey?
Gosh, how naughty.
Never mind that,
it's getting more common by the day."

"I'm sorry, but I really need to ask,
is there another line up after this?
I know I'm here for torture for my sin,
but this is quite the underwhelming twist."

"Are you trying to say something?
The endless mire of administration
isn't torture enough?
That's a bit cheeky.
Were you hoping for something more?

Something far beyond terror?
Is that what you saw yourself deserving?"

"Well no," the Dreamer disagreed,
"for asking questions, wouldn't say deserved.
But I believed that Hell was meant to be
a place where endless punishment was served."

"Punishment? Please.
For asking a few questions?
Where's the justice in that?
You get told your whole life
to be curious,
hold informed beliefs.
You want us to punish you
for questioning a story as big as God?

Nah.

Besides, it's been centuries
since Hell was about torture.
Not since Lucifer,
our Lord of Hell, the Fallen One,
found themself bored with it.
I believe they said
it bummed them out."

This took the Dreamer quite aback,
surprising as it was.

"There's been no punishment for anyone
for all the recent several hundred years?
In all that time, no evil bad enough?"

"I mean, there's always evil,
and they get punished, yeah.
We just send them back in time
to a place where we were more motivated.
We can do that,
dilating time is a specialty for us,
considering time is immaterial here.

But you're not exactly that.
Again, I've read your file.
It's sickeningly pleasant.
So you get the rest of Hell.
Our Lord set it up,
it's all the pleasures of sin,
and you're already in Hell,
so none of the consequences.
What else do you do
to manage the infinite damned
who maybe shouldn't be?"

The Dreamer thought a bit on that.

"I will admit, I'm glad to not be tortured,
but this is still a big surprise to see.

And like you’ve said, I’m not too big on sin.
It doesn’t do a lot of good for me.”

The orange admin demon shrugged.
“Well that one’s up to you.
The party’s always open,
but you’re always welcome
to sit in the corner on your own.
Who knows, at some point in this eternity
you might get bored of virtue.

You can’t stay here with me though.

You’re holding up the line.”

Chapter Three: Poker in the Land of Damnation

“So this was it, could this be it?
Was this the Hell she’d found?
No torture for the sinners here,
Just further depths of debauchery?
A place for further indulgence?
A place for self-exalting?
A place for those who’d just go on,
breaking Heaven’s rules forever?

Well, a lot of those rules,
the Dreamer thought,
were arbitrary.
And they doomed people who,
in her humble opinion,
ought not be doomed.

So then,
if this was all there was to Hell,
May as well join the party.

She didn’t wonder far,
before she was called over to a table.
It held a few other people,
and was set up for a game.

It was helmed by a demon-
but just a little one,
humanoid, short, purple.
Not even a bit of trickery about him.

"You called me over, can I help you pal?"

The little demon held a deck of cards,
and spoke with a voice deeper than midnight.

"I did, I did.
thank you for heeding.
we have a poker game starting-
Hold'em-
we need some extra players."

"I wish I could, but I have never played,
and I only got here not that long ago.
I couldn't offer very much to bet,
I didn't bring my wallet down below."

The poker demon didn't falter.
"Nothing to worry about, nothing at all.
If you've never played,
you'll be awash with Beginner's Luck.
I terms of buy-in,
the only money in Hell
is the great heaping piles of it
we use to crush certain people

who hoarded it in life.
One of those irony things.
No, we bet concepts and ideas here,
and the current buy-in for this table
is one unrealised future
two dreams from childhood,
and a judgement passed on a neighbour's cat."

Which all seemed unconventional,
but also sounded like things
the Dreamer could afford to lose.
'Besides, a first time playing at the table
could be a story I can tell one day.'
And there was that old saying,
'when in Rome.'

So she agreed to join the table,
her buy-in manifesting as floating lights,
converted into piles of chips.
When she sat,
she felt knowledge flood in,
the knowledge of the game;
the infinite essence of uncounted games.
These tables held a certain magic,
and wouldn't want a player to lose,
not for never learning the rules.

Within moments another person sat down,
declaring themself to be 'in'.

This person was unremarkable,
dressed in a regular jacket,
unimpressive trousers,
with the most average frame she'd ever seen.
However she felt from them a powerful sense,
electrifying,
a pure, unmarred charisma.
And their eyes were amber,
such a deep amber,
endless, the way space is endless.

They gave her a smile,
and the poker demon dealt their hands.

'I guess that this would be the setting then,
wherein we'll meet the characters involved,
and probably the conflict of the tale,
a problem that can hopefully be solved.'

As the Dreamer thought this to herself,
the first few hands were played.
Numbers floated around the table,
raised, called, raised and called again.
Little progress made to any wins or losses.

Until someone felt confident,
and made an all-in bet.

'So this would be the story's threshold then,

a challenge a protagonist should meet…
I've got Beginner's Luck to back me up-
I feel like it's too soon to taste defeat.'

The Dreamer called the bet,
confident in her hand,
and trusting the story she told herself.
She wondered then,
what was puffing up Amber-Eyes,
to make them also call?
For the amber-eyed individual did call,
now radiating confidence
and smiling at them all
with the left corner of their mouth.
This changed the table's dynamics
to three all-in players,
and two cowards.

The cowards got to stay in the game though.
The Dreamer's narrative was proven right,
and she entered the game's second act
with a healthy stack of chips,
tied with Amber-Eyes,
as against the odds,
they'd both made the same hand
(two pair, kings and sevens).

"I didn't quite expect a tie.

I guess that means we'll split the pot,"
so said the one with amber eyes,
"that's quite the bit of luck you've got."

The next few hours heated up.
Chips went back and forth,
tumbling around the table.
Amber-Eyes was ahead,
taking hands with precision,
coaxing bets out of otherwise humble players.
Second was one of the other players,
sitting steady on a strategy,
successful but uneventful,
of only taking sure bets.
The Dreamer wasn't far behind,
Luck manifesting as a string of great hands,
buoyed by the story she was telling herself.
The guy in fourth
was in fourth by a lot,
and he was currently all-in on his tiny pile,
which was easily matched
by both the Dreamer and second-place.

The River came,
the guy in fourth revealed three eights,
a reasonable hand,
but beaten by Second's flushed hearts,
and eclipsed by the Dreamer's full house,
queens over fours.

Of course, this win put the Dreamer in last,
as the cast dropped to three,
and the story's act number rose to the same.

By now three hours had passed,
and the poker demon called a break.
"I need a leak,
and a snack would be nice.
Should be about
ten? twenty?
yeah,
Be back in twenty minutes, please."

The Dreamer followed Amber-Eyes,
who headed to a balcony,
and lit a cigarette,
before noticing the Dreamer there.

"So, how you finding it so far?
I heard you haven't played before.
Beginner's Luck is good for that."

The Dreamer caught the condescension,
but that wasn't why she was here.
This person was intriguing,
a well of confidence and charisma.
Still thinking of story,
this must be someone important,

and she had an idea who.

"And after all, in Hell, who matters most?
You've been a total mystery all game.
I think I've figured out just who you are;
Are you the one? Is Lucifer your name?"

And Amber-Eyes,
so far confident and unflappable,
was utterly shocked.

"You recognize I'm in disguise?
Well isn't this a novelty?
I can't believe your human eyes
could spot me in my majesty.

This isn't how they picture me,
the other humans sent to Hell.
They usually expect to see,
the crimson skin, and horns as well.

It's odd then that you'd figure out
that I am Lucifer indeed."

The unremarkable person changed then,
their glamour falling through,
and suddenly they were Lucifer,
Lord of Hell.
Handsome and beautiful,

once Heaven's finest face,
now The Fallen One.

The Dreamer was taken aback,
but still, it was good to be right.
"But why have you been playing in disguise?"

"You figured out my secret name,
but couldn't figure that as well?
I'm trying to avoid the fame
That comes with being Lord of Hell.

You're a clever and insightful one.
I ask you keep it hidden too.
So far the game's been pretty fun.
I hope it's down to me and you."

"I guess that all seems pretty fair to me.
I'm not about to out you here, I swear.
And anyway, the game will go the same,
no matter what the face it is you wear."

And time was up, they went inside,
Lucifer back in their disguise,
to start the last act of the story-
the Dreamer's game had an antagonist now.

With just three players,
the blind bet grew

at very rapid pace.
The Dreamer and Lucifer,
locked on each other now,
nearly forgetting the other player.
It took aggressive betting,
but the two whittled the third player down,
allowing the Dreamer to steal second,
and eventually pricing them out.

Finally it was just the two,
a final conflict for them.
Amazingly matched on chips.
The Dreamer versus the Lord of Hell.

Their hands were dealt
and they both took their looks,
the Dreamer holding pocket sixes.
Blind bets were made,
the Dreamer acted first-
raising their small blind to call.
Lucifer grinned again from the left corner
and agreed to check.

The Flop came,
ace, three, king.
Lucifer raised a pile of chips.
The Dreamer checked her sixes,
and yes, they were still there.
She raised again,

playing on her pair.
Lucifer called with an elevated brow.

The Turn was revealed.
Another king.
All four suits were present on the board,
both were assured a strong pair.
Lucifer chuckled.
“How nice! I think I’ll go all in.”

The Dreamer could fold.
A lesser loss to stay in the game.
But she felt tension in her narrative.

This felt like a good place for a climax,
against the Biggest Bad.
And this was Lucifer,
a schemer and a manipulator.
Wouldn’t it be so like them
to try to win on a bluff?
She had her two pairs,
not the weakest hand.
and as they’d said,
Beginner’s Luck was with her.
She called “all-in.”

They submitted their hands,
face-down on the table,
anticipating the last card.

The River flowed forth,
the six of clubs.

"Beginner's Luck, that's what you said it was.
You tried to beat Beginner's Luck with bluffs?
I call Full House, with sixes over kings.
Your seven-two just isn't strong enough!"

Lucifer's eyebrow climbed an inch up,
their semi-smile curled more,
and they affixed the Dreamer
with their deep amber eyes,
and flipped their cards over.
Both players looked at them,
the seven and two that the Dreamer promised.

"So clever and insightful, yes.
A quite… surprising call.
You saw right through my bluff, I guess.
Well done to you, you win it all!"

Lucifer passed their chips over
and shook the Dreamer's hand.
"I think I'd like to meet again.
For now, there's things I must attend."

And Lucifer, still disguised,
went off through the crowd,

leaving the Dreamer with her win
and no small amount of surprise.

Chapter Four: This Is Why We Keep Good Records, People!

If you've dealt with a bureaucrat,
then surely you must know
the misery of paperwork
continues down below.

The room where all the files are
was infinite in size,
and demons sat and grumbled through
the work we all despise.

The filing demons all snapped to,
the doors swung with a BOOM,
as Lucifer themself strode in,
demanding of the room:

"I need it now! I need her file!
I need to see the things it said!
She's been here just a little while;
She's one of our most recent dead!"

The demons should have moved at once,
but all were struck aghast-

The boss had never stepped in here
in all the eons past.

The shock wore off, they scrambled on
to please their Demon Lord,
and rushed to find the papers in
the mess where they were stored.

“Which one, Excellency?”

“The one from at the gaming table!
The one who won the poker game!”
They cursed that they had been unable
to catch the stranger’s name.

They flexed their hand and conjured up
an image of her face.
“Oh! That was me!” a demon said,
“just let me find my place.”

He searched for just a minute more,
flicked through the morning’s pile,
and eager to appease his Lord,
produced The Dreamer’s file.

And Lucifer, without a blink,
with fire in their eyes,
did tip them for a job well done,
to everyone’s surprise.

"Don't act so shocked, my little friend.
You've done for me what I had asked.
The Lakes will freeze and Hell will end,
before I leave an unpaid task."

(For all of Lucifer's great faults,
They pay their demons well;
They know first hand what happens when
the working class rebel).

Then barricaded in their room,
the Lord began to read,
and what they found upon the page,
"Oh, what an oversight indeed!"

Then Lucifer began to laugh,
with uncontained delight,
and all who heard it pealing out
knew something wasn't right.

Concerned, the Main Advisor was-
she knocked and shouted in,
and Lucifer swung wide the door,
face plastered with a grin.

"My Lord? Are you OK?
I've never heard such mirth from you.
You sound utterly manic."

"My friend, come in," they said with glee,
"You've got no cause to panic".

They pushed The Dreamer's file at her,
perhaps a little rough,
"I knew it in the poker game!
I knew it when she called my bluff!"

But though she studied all of it,
the file answered naught.
What could it be, what was the clue
that she just hadn't caught?

"Your bluff, Excellency?
I'm afraid I don't understand.
Is not bluffing and calling typical of poker?
Even knowing who you are,
to win they'd have to call you eventually".

So Lucifer then sat her down,
a glinting in their eye.
"Then tell me, have you ever known
of me, the Lord of Hell, to lie?"

"Of course", replied the Advisor.
"Like, so many times a day.
You deceive, manipulate,
trick, cajole, misrepresent,
fib and defraud

pretty much everyone."

The Lord of Hell laughed deeply.
"I truly love your honesty.
I thank you then for being true
when talking to my majesty.

You're clearly right. My lies are great,
I trick and cheat, but all the same;
One place I keep the truth on straight
is playing others in a game.

See certain rules, I must obey,
some ancient laws are too concrete;
In games with mortals that I play,
I cannot lie, I cannot cheat.

To break this rule, I never dare.
My skills and luck must be enough.
When playing games I must be fair,
and that's why I will never bluff".

The Chief Advisor took this in.
"Alright", she said, "That's great.
Lord Lucifer is an honest gamer.
Wowee Zowee.
What does this have to do with anything?"

Lord Lucifer slammed down the file,

and with a painted claw,
they pointed out specific lines
with almost rev'rent awe.

"My lovely, have you ever seen
a Dreaming rank as high as ten?
I don't think there has ever been,
or ever will be one again!"

The Chief Advisor shook her head,
she didn't understand.
Why should a Dreaming rank enthrall
the Lord of all the land?

It disappointed Lucifer;
Must they explain it all?
"We live in story, you and I,
and she could soon rewrite it all.

For all that Heaven, all that Hell,
are vast and powerful domains,
but built on thoughts and dreams that swell
inside imaginative brains.

We started out as fictions, dreams,
by people thinking up ideas.
This Dreamer's very strong, it seems.
A Dreaming Rank of ten is clear.

She has a great potential strength,
a power strong and wonderous.
We must attempt, at every length
to make that power work for us".

The Chief Advisor got it then.
"So she's got a strong imagination.
A really strong imagination.
Strong enough to reshape things here?
Could it really be possible?
Can one human make that much change?"

But Lucifer had seen it all,
and they already knew.
"I had the evidence today,
I know the things that she can do.

I told you that I didn't bluff,
in games, I never deal in fiction.
But she believed I do, enough,
believed I would with such conviction.

I had the game, that final round,
paired aces in my hand, I knew.
But when I flipped them, I had found
they'd changed: a seven, and a two.

She told herself I'd lost the game,
so strongly did the girl believe,

the game itself believed the same,
and that was when I had to leave."

Now Lucifer had told it all,
and knew what they would do.
"If I can harness all that strength,
at last my dreams could all come true."

Chapter Five: The Hell-King's Request

A few days since the poker game,
the Dreamer got a call
that Lucifer was seeking her
and waiting in their Hall.

It didn't seem a common thing
as far as she could tell
to get requests to come and see
the Lord of all of Hell.

And wanting something else to do
than poker every day,
she chose to take the offer up
and headed on her way.

The Hall of Lucifer was large
and carved from darkened stone.
The Dreamer found the Fallen One
leant forward on their throne.

"Come in, come in! The poker girl!
I'm just so glad that you could come!
The other day was such a whirl,
I hope you had yourself some fun?"

"It hasn't been that bad so far, I guess.
Not really what I thought that Hell would be."

"You thought there'd be more torture, yes?
The brimstone and the fiery sea?"

"I thought there might be some of it at least,
although I wasn't sure where I'd fit in-
I never thought I'd earned eternal Hell,
considering my life was light on sin."

"You've hit the nail on the head,
that's part of why we mellowed out.
We'd gotten heaps of recent dead
with nothing bad to speak about.

The rules of Heaven got too tight,
too much for people to get in.
We thought it didn't feel too right
to punish those with smaller sins."

The words of Lucifer hit home,
the Dreamer felt a rage,
an anger she'd been simmering,
but holding in a cage.

"I can't believe that asking questions counts,
but that's the only reason that I'm here.

It shouldn't be a sin to ask for proof,
is doubting really such a thing to fear?"

"No doubt you're angry, I can tell.
But here and there, that's how it works.
We function on belief in Hell-
it's just another of our quirks.

See Hell and Heaven both began
in fables told by human minds.
The story spread across the lands
and out of that it all unwinds.

The story told is what we get,
it's human faith that put us here.
So non-believers are a threat,
and no small thing for Gods to fear.

Which brings me to my business here."

The Fallen One produced a file
with flourish and a snap.
The Dreamer recognized her face
upon its outer flap.

"All this is who you used to be,
the file of who you were on Earth.
There's something here for you to see,
a thing that gives you lots of worth."

"It gives me worth, you say? To who? To you?
The stories give you greater charm than this,
they say you're meant to have a silver tongue,
but I am yet to hear the gilded kiss."

So Lucifer apologised,
"I never mean to cause offense,
but get caught up inside my mind.
I know it's not a good defense."

"But look a minute, look at this!"
The Lord of Hell declared,
and pointed to the Dreaming Rank
that had them so ensnared.

"It says I have a Dreaming Rank of ten,
but doesn't give me context for the stat.
You'll have to tell me what the number means
if you want me excited over that."

"I told you that we're story bound,
that you have power over us.
The rank is something that we found
that says that you are dangerous.

A person's Dreaming Rank denotes
their power over story's flow-
the strength of stories that you wrote,

and yours is high as it could go.

In short, if I can make it clear,
your Rank's the highest ever seen.
If you can tap into it here,
you'd rewrite all that's ever been."

Then Lucifer retook their throne,
and watched expectantly,
for if she'd grasp what they had said
and see what she could be.

"I think it seems a little bit far-fetched,
that I could shake the narrative of Hell.
How do you know that what you say is true?
What makes you sure it's me, how can you tell?"

So Lucifer recalled the game,
the way their hand had changed.
"You must have had some power then,
to do a thing so strange.

If you can make yourself believe
the stories written in your head,
imagine what you could achieve
within the worlds of all the dead.

Just try it, tell a simple one.
imagine me a different face.

Make it silly, make it fun,
and write that dream into its place."

The Dreamer chose to humour them,
and so she closed her eyes.

"Once upon a time,
when the depths of Hell were young,
Lucifer, its king, ran headlong into a pole
with the result that their nose grew long,
and their left eye became a purple,
so deep was the bruise to their ego."

The Dreamer held the image still,
and kept it in her mind,
so when she opened up her eyes,
her story did she find.

"You see? It worked! And also, ow!
Did there need to be the pole?
But still, stand up and take a bow,
and step into your magic role."

The Dreamer had some questions though.
"Assuming all the things you've said are true,
I wonder, why would you want me to know?
I wonder, what's the benefit to you?"

"Y'know what, fair enough", they said,

"I have a plan in need of you.
I have a plan to take on God,
a thing that you could help me do.

I'm sure you know, I tried before,
I'm sure you know that's how I fell.
I want to wage another war,
with all the armies damned in Hell.

We've had the battle endless times,
and every time we've been denied,
A Dreamer though, could turn the tides,
could sway the story to my side."

The Dreamer though was horrified.
"Like even if the things you say are true,
I don't think war with Heaven's what I want.
I feel like that's the villain thing to do."

But Lucifer prepared for this,
had planned what they would say.
"I quite agree, the world above
is simply in the way.

My war is not with Heaven, no.
My fight is with its despot God.
The one demanding thoughtless faith,
for entry in the world he's trod.

The one who orders punishment
for simple curiosity,
the wrathful, vain and greedy God.
The one who sent you down to me.

I've seen the souls of Heaven too,
and truly they're no better off.
All sapped of anything but bliss,
their heads all full of fluff.

I'd tip the tyrant from His throne,
His station I would take for me,
and with his power I'd remake
an afterlife where all are free."

"You'd go to Heaven as a saviour then?
To shut down Hell, bring justice to the dead?"
The Dreamer tossed the thought around
and dwelt on what they'd said.

It sounded like a noble goal,
to save the souls of all.
To save the people just like her,
who'd not deserved to fall.

But could she trust the Lord of Hell?
The stories all said no.
The Dreamer needed certainty
of how it all would go.

"You need my narrative to war with God?
Then these will be the terms that I'll accept.
You'll keep me 'round to help you shape the world,
with final say, to which you won't object."

So Lucifer considered this,
and found that they agreed.

"You want to keep my whims in check?
I guess that's fair, I understand.
I'll take the terms you offer me,
to seal the deal, I'll shake your hand."

And so with that, the deal was struck
and Hell would go to war.
A victory was in their grasp
that hadn't been before.

Chapter Six: Tell the Stories Like You Mean Them

"They had their plan, they made a plan,
they had a plan to act.
The armies of Hell had to rally,
the Dreamer had to master the narrative,
to become the backbone of the plan,
to become the story's writer,
to become The Dreamer,
in all her potential."

It was tough going.
Not an easy thing,
for someone who had always told stories,
to make them into truth now.
Part of the fun of it all
was in their lack of consequence.
And Lucifer was never one to nurture.

They wheeled out a pink demon,
chained to a heavy-duty trolley,
with three horns,
a coral-snake tail,
and five arms.
The demon's name was Rupert,
and it was up to the Dreamer

to envision Rupert free of the trolley,
living at home with his wife.

"You need to get your head around,
or you're no good to them or me.
This isn't something you just found,
it's something you were meant to be!

I've seen you do it loads of times,
we know, we both, what you can do,
so it would just be so sublime
if you could try to see it too."

But the Dreamer was being held back,
doubt being a heavier chain
than any holding Rupert down.

"I don't believe that seeing is the issue.
The trouble is, I see a bit too much.
I tell myself that Heaven needs to fall,
but it's a victory I'm scared to touch.

I disagree with why I am condemned,
and you don't seem the villain as foretold,
but raising arms to Heaven's gates?
It seems to me like that's a little bold."

For all that Lucifer was vain,
for all their narcissism,

they were good at reading people.

"You picture Heaven's rightful place
above us waiting down below.
It's fine, I see it in your face,
and trusting me is hard, I know.

But think of what they've done to you,
and know you're not the only one.
we've got a chance here to undo
the damage done to everyone.

And those in Heaven have it worse!
Their lives are so much worse than this,
the bland monotony, the curse
that comes from everlasting bliss.

That's how He keeps them all in line:
He takes their hopes and goals away.
We need, us all, for God Divine
to look upon His final day."

They dressed it up so nobly,
but the Dreamer was unsure,
for she saw a contradiction.

"Is not eternal pleasure what you do?
The endless party, going on in Hell?
Should I believe the two are far apart,

that Lucifer should not be done as well?"

The Dreamer'd been in Hell a while,
and after that first game,
in which she'd won Lucifer's attention,
she'd played a few more.
It got old quickly for her,
and she didn't think the other tables
would offer much excitement-
at least, not an eternal damnation's worth.

"Well therein lies the rub of it;
that counts as torture in its way.
Things lose their luster quite a bit
when they are suffered every day.

I load them up with jewels to hoard,
I give them every kind of treasure,
and given time they all get bored,
unable then to taste the pleasure.

It works the other way as well,
for suffering as well as fun.
The torture that we did in Hell?
Eventually, they all got numb.

It's all a bit insidious,
but I at least don't try to hide.
My Hellish works are hideous,

but I can say I never lied.

Monotony will kill us all,
except that all of us are dead-
and so the system has to fall
a new one needed in its stead.

I need your stories, aye it's true,
to get us through to victory,
but what I really need from you
is dreams of how it all should be."

Lucifer let softness into their voice.
"Will you dream a better afterlife for us all?"

And in answer, the Dreamer dreamed,

"The fiery pits of Hell were blazing,
as its armies readied for war.
But the Demon known as Rupert
was cozy at home,
far from the chains that would bind him."

Behind the Dreamer,
those chains weighed heavily on empty air,
and fell with a clink to the floor.

"I can't just dream a better afterlife,
but I always have the power to believe.

I choose to liberate the afterlife,
a freer one for all can be achieved.

If marching forth to Heaven's what it takes,
then let us go unbolt the Pearly Gates."

Chapter Seven: The War is Fought Again

The Pearly Gates stood tall and strong,
observed by all of Hell,
and seemed to all invincible,
impossible to fell.

To all except for Lucifer,
who turned to them and spoke:
"We've made it here, my legions vast!
Now tell me, has your furor broke?

The Heaven's Gate was wrecked before,
and it was I who did the deed!
And back again, yes back once more-
our strength and might the gates will heed!"

The damned and demons cheered at that,
convictions found again.
The Dreamer's doubts were overcome,
and she believed it then.

So Lucifer took their belief,
and from it forged a spear.
They launched it through the Pearly Gates-
blown wide to raucous cheer.

The battle's prologue ended then,
as through the hole they ran.
With Lucifer at army's front,
the War with Hell began.

On Heaven's side, the Dreamer saw,
an endless wave of souls,
to meet the waves of all the damned,
upon a gilded knoll.

'They seem to have so many more than us-
and as expected, they've all come prepared.
They clearly knew that we were on our way-
but strength for strength, we'll see how they
compare.'

The Dreamer had her moment now,
she knew what dream to weave,
she made a story for herself,
she made herself believe.

'The souls of Heaven have the bigger force,
but Hell is hungry, here for All or Naught.
The damned are buoyed by desperation's sting,
and bolstered by the tortures that they've
fought.'

The damned, infused with Dreamer's will,

fought well against their foe,
with all the tricks and viciousness
they'd picked up down below.

The Dreamer also had to fight,
she couldn't hide away.
With sword at back and shield to hand,
she wouldn't be delayed.

But none compared with Lucifer,
who carved a deathly swarth,
with zero effort in the act
they paved a private path.

A dream of scrappy underdogs-
a classic, if I may.
A common trope so powerful
it might have won the day.

But this was just the opening;
the souls were not alone.
The demons saw another group
that chilled them to the bone.

The air around them came alive.
The ground began to hum.
For these were no mere souls of light.
The Archangels had come.

The opening was over now,
for though they're low in rank,
the angels far outstripped the damned,
and so their chances sank.

But Lucifer had planned for this,
had waited for the beat.
"The angels have no time for you!
There's demons here for them to meet!

Behold, the creatures born in Hell!
The twisted fiends of darkest minds!
I think they'll match your angels well,
They're quite a force, I think you'll find."

On hearing this, the Dreamer turned
and saw the demons shriek.
"What products of the sickest minds are these?
I never could've dreamed a dream so bleak."

They were all designed to terrify,
a brief they met with glee,
all born of swirling nightmare stuff,
from which all men would flee.

A lot of them were leathery,
but some were smoke or flame,
and others yet were made of rock,
no two of them the same.

A lot of them were humanoid,
as close as they could make.
A few resembled animals;
some birds, some dogs, a snake.

Some too much tooth, some too few eyes,
and most of them with wings.
But all of them protruding bones
designed for stabbing things.

The angels saw these things approach
and rushed to push them back,
and as the armies clashed again
the skies began to crack.

The Dreamer stuck to pushing on-
she couldn't bear to look.
To see these monsters on her team,
her confidence was shook.

She chose instead to move along.
As Lucifer had said:
they'd win if they could reach the throne,
without it they'd be dead.

And Lucifer kept pushing forth,
through soul and angel each.
They tore asunder anyone

they found within their reach.

"My demons match your angels, Lord!
The damned will overrun your souls!
I must be frank, I'm getting bored
of winning on the gilded knoll!

This isn't it, bring out your best!"
They jeered with violent glee.
"You've seen me tearing up the rest,
I thought you'd have a fight for me!"

A big mistake, the Dreamer thought.
"It can't bode well, to say those things out loud.
We haven't seen their strongest forces yet,
What terrors will you bring, so vain and proud?"

As if in answer, Heaven thrummed.
The sky was washed with green,
and hence there came a reckoning
beyond what yet they'd seen.

From everywhere a chorus rang,
a holy noise so clear,
for Heaven now had sent its best;
the Seraphim were here.

Bedecked in light, and helmed with wings,
no eyes, but seeing all-

They radiated with a sense
that all of Hell would fall.

The mightiest of angels twitched.
The air itself convulsed.
Then with a shriek that split the realms
they leased a deathly pulse.

A devastating wave of light
washed over friend and foe
erasing each and everyone
who met its awful glow.

Assuming that her time had come,
the Dreamer bowed her head,
and wondered what would happen when
she died already dead.

But Lucifer would not have that.
They ran to Dreamer's side.
They took her shoulder in their hand,
above the noise they cried:

"You can't believe the end is near!
You know what happens if you do.
So raise your chin and stow your fear,
and trust that what I say is true!

You know that I'm the Lord of Hell,

and all its power comes from me.
That strength returns from all who fell,
To I who caused it all to be.

Believe in this, and we'll succeed.
There's not a chance for us to lose.
The power's all but guaranteed,
and we'll create the world we choose."

The Dreamer looked to Lucifer
and knew their words were true.
The cut-down might of Hell came back
and to its owner flew.

"I told you so, you shouldn't doubt.
My human friend, it's you and me.
It's time to take the garbage out,
the final chapter's here, you'll see."

They turned and eyed the Seraphim.
The air around them bent,
then like a popping cork, they flew,
with murderous intent.

The Dreamer whispered to herself,
"I needed you to keep me thinking straight.
They say you lie, but I would call them dreams.
Now go and prove that narrative has weight."

The Seraphim faced Lucifer.
"I'll see you bow to Hell's Great Lord!"
They manifested all their strength
into a blazing sword.

They swung it at a Seraphim,
and with it did they rend
two halves of Heaven's highest rank,
now shown its grizzly end.

And though the angels had no mouths,
the Dreamer heard them curse.
For every one the Hell-King struck,
their payback would be worse.

But armed with all the fires of Hell,
the Fallen One cared not.
"You'll stop me not with empty threats!
Then come, and show me what you've got!"

But Seraphim have earned their rank,
they met the Hell-King's test.
An even war was waged that day,
for God had sent His best.

No longer did the Dreamer fear.
"If this is where they make their final stand,
a story hates a battle won too fast.

The clash twixt Hell and Heaven should be
Grand.

The story has to favour both of us,
Our hearts've come with altruistic goals .
The story wants a hero's victory,
What better could there be than saving souls?

This cruelty, this awful, petty God
this coward hiding on His holy throne-
a tyrant here must meet the end He's earned,
must reap the righteous fury that He's sown."

What were the Seraphim to do
with such conviction faced?
With one last push from Lucifer
they found their resting place.

The War with Hell was almost done.
Both sides had lost a toll.
The Dreamer and the Lord of Hell
alone upon the knoll.

Chapter Eight: What To Do When Ambition Outstrips Ability?

A victory seemed well assured
as just the two remained-
the Dreamer and the Fallen One
alone amongst the slain.

They'd trusted in the tale they told
and made it manifest.
They knew their faith would hold them through
to face the final test.

Until the Voice of Heaven spoke.
"Delightfully done, is that the end?
You've woven quite the epic war,
my Fallen One.
Now…

Will you do it all again?"

The second that the Voice was done,
the knoll was full of lives,
as all who'd fallen on the day
were suddenly revived.

As if they hadn't been destroyed,
as if they hadn't fought.
The Dreamer's efforts, all in vain.
The war had been for nought.

Again the armies poised to fight
the damage all undone,
and faced with such futility
the Dreamer longed to run.

But Lucifer would not be cowed.
"We did it once, O' Holy One!
Your power doesn't have me wowed,
we'll fight until the battle's done!"

The Dreamer watched as He came forth.
She knew not what she saw.
To finally see God up close;
her heart was washed with awe.

From Him she felt amazing things,
as if she saw his heart.
Emotions ebbing forth from Him,
and she felt every part.

"You cannot end the cycle now,
you arrogant and pompous fool!
You brought them back to die again?

It's only you who'd be so cruel."

'Except,' the Dreamer realised,
'I feel no anger, sense no bit of spite.
For such a vengeful, cruel and nasty God,
there's nothing in Him wanting for a fight.'

"You would have your fight, Lucifer?
You would fight for eternity?"

And Lucifer's response was quick,
such venom did it hold,
he hissed it in a whispered bite
so vicious and so cold.

"You'll not stop me, my Lord of All.
So long as there is life in me,
though endless times you'll make me fall,
I'll fight until we're all set free."

"You say as such, you say as such.
But you trespass on the Gilded Knoll.
It would take nothing from me,
not a thing,
to send your army back
whence it came"

"Send us back to Hell, my Lord,
we'll be back at the Pearly Gates.

Enough to keep us from reward?
I can't conceive of such a fate."

The Dreamer heard it all, and thought
'It seems they have an even stalemate.
He'll send them back to Hell on endless loop
and they'll come back to satisfy their hate.'

But then, the Dreamer thought, "unless",
and as the thought came forth,
"Well that's an idea, isn't it?
Your friend has it figured out.
A Dreamer, I see.
How nice for you."
The Dreamer sensed a sadness then,
but not from whom she thought.

"What thought have you just stolen then?
What vicious, nasty piece of spite?
You think that you can stop me, friend?
What fancy takes your cruel delight?"

Then Lucifer's deep eyes went wide,
they caught the Dreamer's eye.
"He'll smite us all. So that's his plan.
Our very sense of self will die.

We'll be erased from History,
removed as if we'd never been.

So that's the thought you took from her!
So that's the story's end you've seen!"

"Ah Lucifer, Oh Lucifer.
Sweet Lucifer.
Smite you?
Nay, I'll not do that.
What fairness would that be,
to punish you for acting
the way your creator built you?
No, no, no.
You want to fight a forever war?
Then I shall hold you here in amber,
this moment stretched eternally,
a private war for Lucifer Morningstar."

The Fallen caught the Dreamer's eye again
"Remember all the things I've said!
This liar's mind will shift again,
He'd love to see our armies dead!"

"I have no wish to kill you, Lucifer.
But as you seem so intent,
as you seem to insist…"

'It's true, it seems the word's 'insist' indeed.
Is Lucifer too obstinate to feel?
There isn't any viciousness at all,
and yet they still insist on this appeal.'

"As you seem to insist,
I suppose I can try-
I can attempt to erase you
remove the Lord of Hell from the fable."

"You see that, Dreamer, do you see?
I told you what this God would do!"

And 'Yes', the Dreamer thought, 'you did.
You said it to me many, many times.
Many times, you said this God was cruel,
a worm that dug its way into my mind.'

God heard her thoughts and felt surprise,
and Lucifer said "NO!"
The Dreamer looked upon them both.
Her eyes began to glow

"I rather think there's been enough of this,"
the Dreamer said out loud.
She wove another story then,
a sermon to the crowd:

"In the end, there was nothing.
And all was dark.
And into that void stepped three people…"

Chapter Nine: The Dreamer's Turn at the Fable

"In the end, there was nothing.
And all was dark.
And into that void stepped three people
untethered from the narrative,
outside of their grand mythological roles,
and lacking any power,
except to talk freely
or leave."

The Dreamer sat on a chair of dreamstuff,
and breathed in deep
waiting for the other two to do the same
and creating room for her thoughts.

The other two,
the Lords of Hell and Heaven,
surveyed her
but neither could speak.
God, because He was patient.
Lucifer, because they were unsure.
God, because He was grateful.
Lucifer, because they were afraid.

"You tricked me, then.

You never aimed to topple God.
Not with this fight at least."

A glint struck up in Lucifer's eye
and their smile curled a little.
"It was a possible contingency.
I wouldn't have said no to it.
With Dreaming on our side?
It could have been."

"But no, you're right.
Primarily I hoped to die."

Like a wild bear,
Lucifer growled then.
"You've known the curse of monotony.
I showed it to you,
and you begged to be freed.
Imagine being caught,
being mired in that,
for eternity.
Imagine knowing that no matter what,
there would always be another tomorrow."

The Dreamer wasn't having it.
She might have felt pity for Lucifer,
if there was room next to the sudden disdain-
the pathetic truth of Lucifer laid bare.
"You used me.

Made me trust you and fed me lies.
Told me you wanted a better tomorrow,
while wanting to never see one again?"

"And just like the war,
I'd do it again, and again.
As many tomorrows as it takes.
Humans have romanticized tomorrow.
Another day of experience,
another second chance.
These can only be pleasant dreams
if they don't stretch on forever.
Infinite tomorrow,
it mocks the idea of the future,
makes miserable todays,
and erodes the joy of the past."

Lucifer glowered at God,
a reprimanded child
regretting not their actions,
but being caught.
"I want my last tomorrow.
You locked me into my role.
How truly cruel are you?"

But the Dreamer had felt His sadness.
A sadness that cruelty has no space for,
and she knew the answer to it.
She opened space for Him.

"You're right.
I made the role for you.
I pushed you into it,
made you the Lord of Hell.
You had raged against me,
and I was vengeful, I won't deny.

We didn't know then
the way we do now,
what would happen to a story
once it became codified.

Then even Hell was twisted,
changed from my intent.
I needed a place of reform
a place people could grow,
even after death,
before finding their way to Heaven.
A world of torture?
A place of punishment?
What interest would I have in that?
But fables work in black and white,
and if Heaven was for the good,
Hell then must be a prison for evil.

I never meant for this to be forever.
But our story, our myth,
it caught too many minds

There was no erasing the narrative.
By the time I regretted my choice,
it was immutable backstory."

This all made sense in theory.
In practice though
the Dreamer didn't believe.
"Are you not God?
You're not more powerful than story?
I felt your sadness earlier.
No matter what I was told,
no matter how many times,
I couldn't write you into cruelty."

God laughed at that,
a deeply warm sound.
"No wonder you both got on so well.
That's a healthy dose of arrogance!
You write a strong story, Dreamer.
Very strong.
But strong as one told across the world?

I exist in so many hearts,
in so many minds.
I am a story told over thousands of years.
There's too much power in that
for any God to break from."

Lucifer had to ask,

despite themself,
curiosity getting their better,
with a touch of pithiness,
“Her power works on me.
I’m in all those stories too,
your other side,
the villain defining you.
So what, you’re special?
A God too strong to be rewritten,
too weak to break free of what’s written?”

“If I had to guess,” answered God,
“and it’s odd that I do have to guess,
I’d say it’s in the telling.
I, me, God-
it’s a consistent characterisation.
How do you see me, Dreamer?
How do I appear to you?
I’ll take an easy assumption;
As a man, older,
white haired and bearded,
plainly robed?

Of course you do.
That’s the face I’ve worn so much
across ages and across cultures.
The myth of me is concrete.

But you, Lord of Hell?

How many names do you wear?
How many faces?
The story of Hell's King is mercury.
Are you Lucifer?
Are you Satan?
Beelzebub, Diablo, Old Nick?
Sometimes these are separate entities,
and sometimes interchanged.
So many 'The Devils' across the world.
A different myth to any and all,
of course you fell into this one so easily."

This made sense to the three of them.
The kind of sense
that was too much sense to be false.
So they sat and contemplated.

Then the Dreamer had a question.
Not a world-shattering one.
Nothing about the role of gods or devils.
No ponderance of narrative power.
Just a combination of curiosity
and unobserved courtesy.
"So what name do you take then?
What would you like us to call you?"

And He was surprised,
a rare treat.
"No name I gave myself, for sure.

I suppose- I guess-
I've never considered it, actually.
They know what I am when they see me,
so nobody ever asks.
There are a few names that people give me.
But one I'd choose for myself?
I think…
I think you'll have to give me time."

"I've got a couple names for you,"
Lucifer muttered.
They stood up, hands on hips,
sighed a defeated sigh
and wiped a hand across their face
as if to pull their weariness out.
"So what now then?
Do we return?
Head back to the story and submit?
Drift in its depths again and again?"

Their voice raised,
no anger left to hide the desperation.
"Is tomorrow just another day?
Will you force me to fight you forever,
unable to let either of us end?
Does the fable so desperately need a villain?"

And finally,
as Lucifer dropped a tear,

the Dreamer felt pity move in.
There had to be something to do.
And it came to her, of course.

The Dreamer was good at dreaming.

"The fable needs a Lucifer-
the story needs its villain.
It needs a Satan, a devil.
That seems immutable.
But does the fable need you?
There's a way out for everyone,
everyone not named Lucifer, at least."

She asked again.
"So what name would you take then?
What would you like us to call you?"

And they who once were Lucifer,
(before their role was shed)
grew joyful as they realised
just what the Dreamer said.

The Dreamer dreamed them something new,
the renamed Lord of Hell.
They got a brand new story, but
it's one we'll never tell.

Then she and God stayed there a bit,

just chatting in the peace.
And so the Dreamer's story ends-
this part of it, at least.

Epilogue: The Teller and the Voice of Stories Wrap it Up

"So then. Well then.
Righto then.
That's where we're ending the story.
It's not where they all finish up.
Not where the Dreamer ends up
not where their lives are over,
not even the end of that day,
with nothing else going on."

But we aren't spilling anything,
not telling any more.
You'll have to trust that all involved
have lots of life in store.

But none of that's for you to know,
no matter how you fuss.
The narrative is theirs alone-
a courtesy from us.

We won't encode what happens next,
won't set their lives in stone.
In doing this we hope their lives
will just be theirs alone.

"Hey, don't ask me, don't look at me,
don't think I'll spill the beans.
I won't give voice to anything either.
You're welcome to imagine it though,
to picture what they all do next,
to picture the roles they step into,
to picture your own continuation,
engage with the story, give it a life."

"See honestly, yes honestly,
to be honest with you
They'd probably prefer that you do.
The next chapter in your head is unique.
A separate story from mine,
A separate story from your neighbour's,
A separate story from anyone's,
not concrete or definitive."

To make a story canonized,
it's not the hardest stakes.
A thousand dreamers dreaming one
is often all it takes.

A thousand dreaming separately?
Well then, the tale is free.
So many different truths to hear;
why, which one could it be?

"We told you, see we told you,

yes, we told you we'd not say.
I think you'll agree that it's best.
The Dreamer gets to go on,
and it's your turn to say where,
it's your turn to plot the course,
It's your turn.
Your turn at the fable, now."

But where then does that leave us all,
if now we're at the end?
What happens when you close the book,
will you still hear us, friend?

We Tell and Voice the stories, yes,
but we're a story too.
And when you reach the end of us,
what will we mean to you?

Well thanks for staying here a while
That's all we've got to say.
But if you like, we'd love if you'd
come back another day.

"So long to you, farewell to you.
Auf wiedersehen, goodbye.
You've been a wonderful audience.
Cheers for letting us be with you.
Thanks for hearing us.
Thanks for taking the stories in.

Thanks for keeping us alive,
through just one story more."

Although, Then Again

Maybe just one more, for the road?

The Encore is the Start of Something New

Unlimited stories are being respun,
the universe picks out a strand,
and suddenly your little story's begun,
a narrative sure to be grand.

It starts as a weaving together of lives,
two threads brought together as one,
and breathed into them, a chance to survive
the warmth of a glowing new sun.

So Once Upon a Time you start,
and out of that your story flows.
We've gotten you a central part,
we're watching how the story goes.

A Teller's something that you'll need,
to track the story as you grow.
to chronicle your starting deeds
for when you're old enough to know.

And someone else to be your Voice,
until you get to find your own.
They'll have to speak for every choice
and want you have before you've grown.

You'll meet a cast of characters,
who'll place the world and settings down.
Within your first opening chapters
There's lots of groundwork to be found.

That's how it's gonna be at first
a whole new world just pushed at you,
delivered to you in a burst
of life you'll have to see and do.

And someone else directs your tale-
the very early parts at least-
while you're too young to burn a trail-
before your writing skills increase.

By gosh I have to wonder then,
What parts of it'll stay with you.
What steps will you remember when
the narrative returns to you?

So then, when your prologue's done-
I wonder what comes after that.
What pathway will your story run?
What plots and threads will knot and plait?

Which other people join your cast?
What challenges will come your way?
What stories told by people past,

will make and shape your every day?

What goals will you be aiming for?
Which kinds of villains will you face?
What twists and turns will be in store?
How fast will be your story's pace?

I'm sure there's work you'll copy from,
there's work by which you'll be inspired,
to write besides and rhyme along-
They'll be the sparks that light your fire.

And what a fire it'll be,
how bright a story you will spin.
It's one that we can't wait to see,
we're eager for it to begin.

Printed by Libri Plureos GmbH in Hamburg, Germany

9 789358 737455